What Every Teacher
Should Know About

The Profession and Politics of Teaching

What Every Teacher Should Know About ...

What Every Teacher Should Know About
Diverse Learners

What Every Teacher Should Know About
Student Motivation

What Every Teacher Should Know About
Learning, Memory, and the Brain

What Every Teacher Should Know About
Instructional Planning

What Every Teacher Should Know About
Effective Teaching Strategies

What Every Teacher Should Know About
Classroom Management and Discipline

What Every Teacher Should Know About
Student Assessment

What Every Teacher Should Know About
Special Learners

What Every Teacher Should Know About
Media and Technology

What Every Teacher Should Know About
The Profession and Politics of Teaching

DONNA WALKER TILESTON

What Every Teacher Should Know About
The Profession and Politics of Teaching

CORWIN PRESS
A Sage Publications Company
Thousand Oaks, California

For information:

Corwin Press
A Sage Publications Company
2455 Teller Road
Thousand Oaks, California 91320
www.corwinpress.com

Sage Publications Ltd.
6 Bonhill Street
London EC2A 4PU
United Kingdom

Sage Publications India Pvt. Ltd.
B-42, Panchsheel Enclave
Post Box 4109
New Delhi 110 017 India

Printed in the United States of America

Library of Congress Cataloging-in-Publication Data

Tileston, Donna Walker.
What every teacher should know about the profession and politics
of teaching / Donna Walker Tileston.
     p. cm. — (What every teacher should know about— ; 10)
Includes bibliographical references and index.
ISBN 0-7619-3126-0 (paper)
    1. Teaching—United States—Handbooks, manuals, etc. 2.
Teachers—United States—Handbooks, manuals, etc. I. Title. II. Series.
LB1775.2.T56 2004
371.1—dc21   2003013219

This book is printed on acid-free paper.

        04   05   06   10   9   8   7   6   5   4   3

Acquisitions Editor:	Faye Zucker
Editorial Assistant:	Stacy Wagner
Production Editor:	Diane S. Foster
Copy Editor:	Kris Bergstad
Typesetter:	C&M Digitals (P) Ltd.
Proofreader:	Mary Meagher
Indexer:	Molly Hall
Cover Designer:	Tracy E. Miller
Production Artist:	Lisa Miller

Contents

About the Author

Donna Walker Tileston, Ed.D., is a veteran teacher of 27 years and the president of Strategic Teaching and Learning, a consulting firm that provides services to schools throughout the United States and Canada. Also an author, Donna's publications include *Strategies for Teaching Differently: On the Block or Not* (Corwin Press, 1998), *Innovative Strategies of the Block Schedule* (Bureau of Education and Research [BER], 1999), and *Ten Best Teaching Practices: What Brain Research, Learning Styles and Standards Say About Learning* (Corwin Press, 2000), which has been on Corwin's best-seller list since its first year in print.

Donna received her B.A. from the University of North Texas, her M.A. from East Texas State University, and her Ed.D. from Texas A & M University-Commerce. She may be reached at www.strategicteachinglearning.com or by e-mail at dwtileston@yahoo.com.

Acknowledgments

My sincere thanks go to my Acquisitions Editor, Faye Zucker, for her faith in education and what this information can do to help all children be successful. Without Faye, these books would not have been possible.

I had the best team of editors around: Diane Foster, Stacy Wagner, and Kris Bergstad. You took my words and you gave them power. Thank you.

Thanks to my wonderful Board Chairman at Strategic Teaching and Learning, Dulany Howland: Thank you for sticking with me in the good times and the tough spots. Your expertise and friendship have been invaluable.

*To Sandi Darling, who has been my mentor and
cherished friend throughout this project.*

Introduction

May you live in exciting times.

—Jewish Proverb

This is an exciting time in education. Never before have we had access to so much information about how the brain learns and remembers. Yet, never before have we been under a magnifying glass held by the stakeholders in education as we are at this time. If the now-famous Coleman Report on the state of education was a cry for reform, it might be said that the current mood and legislation before us is a shout for results.

Teachers are leaving the teaching field in droves, not just because of the low pay but also because of the lack of discipline, the demands on time and energy, and the politics involved in trying to please so many. Teachers enter the teaching field without being given the hidden agenda for survival. No wonder the average teacher today leaves teaching within the first five years. The first-year teacher is often shown to a room, handed some textbooks, and left to figure the rest out.

If teachers were paid merely to convey information directly from their texts to their students, we would not have a teacher shortage; as we all know, however, teaching involves much more time, effort, and commitment. We must begin to provide scaffolding for teachers so that they can build a strong foundation before we leave them on their own. Mentoring is a step in the right direction, but it is limited by the quality of the mentor and the new teacher's ability to ask the right questions.

This book is offered as a guide to help new and veteran teachers provide the scaffolding for success. Caine and Caine asked this question in 1997 and could well ask the same question today: "Is there something functioning at an even deeper level that makes sense of the conflict and crisis, and that gives us a handle on how to approach the enormous problems we face?" It is time to answer the question.

One of the most important things we can do for our students today is to teach them the vocabulary they will need to be successful in the lessons and assessments given. Teach vocabulary first and see what a difference it makes. I am modeling what I say. In Form 0.1 are the vocabulary words needed for this book. In the column "Your Definition," write in your understanding of the word at this time. After you have read the book, see if you have changed your mind about your definition or if you want to enhance your first thoughts about the words. I am also including a vocabulary pre-test for you to assess your understanding at this time.

Form 0.1   Vocabulary List for the Profession and Politics of Teaching

Vocabulary Term	Your Definition	Revised Definition
Academic learning time		
Accountability		
Alignment		
Assessment		
Burnout		
Criterion-referenced		
Due process		
Effective school correlates		
Formative assessment		
Inservice training		
Learning community		
No Child Left Behind Act		
Norm-referenced test		
Paraprofessional		
Parenting styles		
Performance-based instruction		
Planning		
Professional growth		
Reflective practitioner		
School culture		
Summative assessment		
Teacher empowerment		
Teaching style		
Title I		
Title VI		
Title VII		
Title IX		

Vocabulary
Pre-Test

Instructions: Choose the best answer or answers for each of the questions provided.

1. Monroe School has a planning session set for Friday so that teachers and community members can examine the school's progress in terms of alignment. This means that the group will be examining . . .
   A. Assessment instruments
   B. Curriculum
   C. Legal safeguards
   D. Instructional practices

2. The work of the effective school movement still remains with us today. Which of the following is not one of the correlates?
   A. Instructional leadership
   B. Direct instruction
   C. Frequent assessment of student progress
   D. A mission statement

3. When we assess declarative objectives, we are assessing . . .
   A. Facts
   B. Processes
   C. Projects
   D. Vocabulary

4. The time that our students are on task and engaged in the learning is called . . .
   A. Allocated time
   B. School time
   C. Academic learning time
   D. Resource time

5. The reason most teachers leave the field is . . .
   A. Money
   B. Burnout
   C. Time constraints
   D. They do not know their subject matter

6. A parent who adheres to a rigid set of rules that apply in every circumstance shows which type of parenting style?
   A. Permissive–indifferent
   B. Authoritarian
   C. Permissive–indulgent
   D. Authoritative

7. A person who works under the supervision of the regular teacher but is not accredited to teach in the classroom is called a . . .
   A. Paraprofessional
   B. Parent
   C. Special programs teacher
   D. Student

8. Ms. McComas just completed a parent–teacher conference about the behavior of one of her students in class. The student is often off task or daydreaming during instruction. The parents were not concerned and informed Ms. McComas that time would take care of the problem. Which parenting style did they demonstrate?
   A. Permissive–indulgent
   B. Authoritarian
   C. Permissive–indifferent
   D. Authoritative

9. During Mr. Walker's first year of teaching, his classroom was visited several times by his principal in 15-minute "walk-throughs." In addition, Mr. Walker was required to turn in all assessment instruments that he used in his classroom along with lesson plans. Mr. Walker's principal is involved in . . .
   A. Formative assessment
   B. Teacher empowerment
   C. Reflection
   D. Summative assessment

10. Which of the following are major categories in the No Child Left Behind Act of 2001?
    A. School choice
    B. Quality teachers
    C. Assessment
    D. Greater funding

11. This act makes it illegal to discriminate in regard to race, color, or national origin in any program that receives federal funding.
    A. Title I
    B. Title VII
    C. Title IX
    D. Title VI

12. This act is sometimes called the Bilingual Act.
    A. Title I
    B. Title VII
    C. Title IX
    D. Title VI

13. This act makes it illegal to discriminate on the basis of gender.
    A. Title I
    B. Title VII
    C. Title IX
    D. Title VI

14. Polly's state test is a test over the standards passed by her state for the fourth grade. Polly's score will be based on whether or not she shows mastery of the given set of objectives. Polly's test is . . .
    A. A norm-referenced test
    B. An IQ test
    C. A criterion-referenced test
    D. An aptitude test

15. Polly's teacher develops the classroom goals around state standards. Polly's teacher has provided a list of procedural objectives. Which of the following objectives would *not* be a procedural objective?
    A. Students will know the vocabulary terms.
    B. Students will create a graphic organizer.
    C. Students will identify the main characters in the story.
    D. Students will write a second ending to the story.

16. Ms. Alvarez has her final review with her principal today to determine the status of her contract. This is called . . .
    A. A formative evaluation
    B. A summative evaluation
    C. Due process
    D. A reflective assessment

17. Mr. Denali provided his students with a list of declarative objectives for their unit on fractions. Which of the following would not be a declarative objective?
    A. Students will understand the vocabulary words identified with fractions.
    B. Students will compare and contrast fractions and decimals.
    C. Students will work problems using fractions.
    D. Students will create their own word problems using fractions.

18. Most state tests are tests of . . .
    A. Procedural objectives
    B. Declarative objectives
    C. Intelligence
    D. Standards

19. Under the No Child Left Behind Act, teachers must . . .
    A. Demonstrate that they know their subject area
    B. Be fully certified
    C. Demonstrate their teaching abilities to a mentor
    D. Serve on decision-making committees

20. Being a good planner means that the teacher plans for . . .
    A. Student behaviors
    B. Teacher behaviors
    C. Student objectives
    D. Strategies for teaching

1

The Politics of Teaching

In January 2002, President Bush signed into law the No Child Left Behind Act, which was heralded as the most significant education reform in decades. The bill came as an answer to the demands of the stakeholders in education to demonstrate quality through a variety of means. Education has been under the magnifying glass since its inception, with sweeping bills and orders making improvements with each decade. It is no surprise that the No Child Left Behind Act (2001) also makes sweeping changes, beginning with accountability. In this chapter, we will examine the four main aspects of the bill—accountability and testing, flexible use of federal resources, school choice, and quality teachers and teaching—and the implications for you as a classroom teacher.

ACCOUNTABILITY AND TESTING

Accountability is not a new issue in education; where this bill is different is that it calls for more standardized testing than ever before. Why so much testing? Perhaps because so many outside the education community consider testing to be a way to measure success. The bill calls for annual testing in reading and mathematics for students in Grades 3–8 beginning in the 2005–2006 school year. The bill goes a step farther by requiring states and schools to break down their test data into subgroups to ensure that all students are making progress regardless of ethnicity, race, gender, or economic status. Each group should be making adequate yearly progress. In the past, schools with low ratios of minorities or low instances of poverty could show high test scores simply because the majority group's scores were high enough to offset a sub-group's low scores. When subgroups are examined separately, students are less likely to fall through the cracks. By the year 2013–2014, all students must meet or exceed the proficiency level in mathematics and reading.

Implications for the Classroom Teacher

Accountability today means that teachers must become familiar with standards set by their states for student learning. Figure 1.1 is a diagram of how an aligned instructional program works. At the top of the triangle stands the written curriculum from which we teach. At the heart of that written curriculum should be a set of standards that clearly shows what students need to know (declarative objectives) and be able to do (procedural objectives) as a result of the learning. You can go to your state Website to look at the standards for what you teach.

The second part of the triangle is what we teach. What we teach in the classroom should be directly connected to the state and local goals at the top of the triangle. That means everything that we teach should have a link to state and local standards. If I am teaching students about the Romantic Period in literature or teaching elementary students about weather patterns, I must be able to show the stakeholders the standard that is being met.

The third part of the triangle is assessment. If I am teaching to standards, I should also be testing to standards. That means my teaching plan should directly relate (and list) the standard,

Figure 1.1   An Aligned Instructional Program

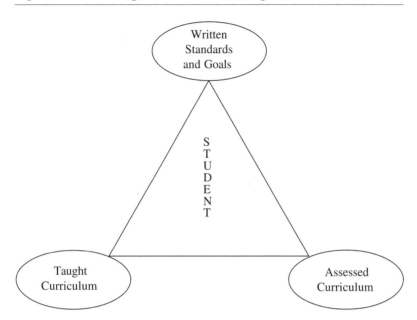

my teaching goals, what I am teaching, and how I am teaching it, and the assessment should directly reflect that teaching. I suggest that teachers send this information home to parents or make it available in communications with parents, students, and colleagues.

Wiggins and McTighe (1998) suggest writing the assessment first. What do you want students to know and be able to do as a result of the learning? By writing the assessment or rubric first, the likelihood is greater that the assessment truly reflects the curriculum.

Accountability means that classroom teachers keep accurate and up-to-date records so that they can back up grades, notes, behavior questions, and the like. What Every Teacher Should Know About Instructional Planning (Tileston, 2004b) has examples of ways that the classroom teacher can keep records on all students in a concise and workable format.

Accountability means that the classroom teacher adequately prepares students for all assessments, including state and national tests. And, no, I did not just imply that we should teach to the test—that would cover only surface knowledge, and we want far more for our students! What I am advising is to teach the information that will make students successful on the test.

If you have read my other books, such as *What Every Teacher Should Know About Learning, Memory, and the Brain* (2004c), you know that motivation is largely influenced by self-efficacy. Self-efficacy is the belief that you can be successful because you have demonstrated success in the past. This belief is much more powerful than self-esteem because it is built on fact, on the old adage that success breeds success. We want and need our students to be successful on state and national assessments. They must be in order to take the next step to grade levels, graduation, entrance into the next field, and so on. How do we teach them what is needed on the test? Besides teaching the skills and facts needed to master the test, there is a silver bullet to bringing up test scores now. Here it is: Teach the vocabulary of the test. An example taken from the learning standards for Texas for eighth-grade mathematics follows:

Patterns, relationships, and algebraic thinking. The student identifies proportional relationships in problem situations and solves problems. The student is expected to:

(A) compare and contrast proportional and nonproportional relationships; and

(B) estimate and find solutions to application problems involving percents and proportional relationships such as similarity and rates.

Some vocabulary that I would teach my students directly include:

- Compare and contrast
- Proportional relationships (including similarity and rates)

- Non-proportional relationships

- Estimate

- Application

- Percentage

Some strategies that I know from the research (see *What Every Teacher Should Know About Instructional Planning*, Tileston, 2004b) will help my students with this vocabulary include:

- Teach students to build compare-and-contrast models.

- Teach vocabulary using proven methods for teaching.

- Teach students to build attribute models and Mind Maps.

- Use scaffolding.

If you want to know more about how to teach the vocabulary of your state test, go to www.learningbridges.com and look at the sample items on this powerful Website or look at my own Website at www.strategicteaching&learning.com

The fourth implication is that there will be more testing in general and more high-stakes testing. As a teacher, you can help your students lower their anxiety level over testing by lowering your anxiety level. Teach them well and prepare them based on the standards you are given and then instill confidence in them that they know the information.

Richard Bandler (1988), who was the co-discoverer of neurolinguistic programming, says that our brain has three criteria that must be filled in order for it to "know what it knows": (1) The information must be reinforced in the learner's preferred modality (visual, auditory, or kinesthetic); (2) the information must be reinforced for the correct number of times (for some that is once and for others it may be multiple times); and (3) the information must be reinforced for a sufficient length of time (for some a matter of seconds and for others, multiple minutes).

FLEXIBLE USE OF FEDERAL RESOURCES

In their policy brief on No Child Left Behind, Cicchinelli, Gaddy, Lefkowits, and Miller (2003) say that appropriations for this bill fall "$5.3 billion short of the authorized funding levels for the Act." More and more educators are mandated to do more in terms of accountability and reform without the tax dollars to support such efforts. When mandates are made without the funding to carry them out, money must come from somewhere. It is hoped that great thought is put into identifying what works and what does not and that resources are shifted to those programs that are working. This is not always the case, however, and important programs may be cut. Class size may increase, and teachers may be reassigned to another campus or their contracts not renewed. Schools, districts, and state educators need to formulate a plan and timeline for improvement, and they need to share that plan with all of the stakeholders, including the teachers and students who are most affected by change. Cicchinelli and colleagues (2003) quote a significant study by the RAND company:

> In an analysis of the cost-effectiveness of various reform initiatives to enhance student achievement, RAND researchers (Grissmer, Flanagan, Kawatta, & Williamson, 2000) found that the cost-effectiveness of specific strategies can vary according to the circumstances of a state's students. For instance, in states with high proportions of disadvantaged students, lowering student-teacher ratios in grades 1–4 can lead to a statewide score gain of approximately three percentile points per student, at a statewide per-student cost of $150. To achieve the same gain in a state that serves predominately middle-SES students, the per-student cost rises to $450. Notably, however, providing teachers with increased funds for instructional materials and other teaching resources at a statewide per-pupil cost of as little as $110 results in the same three percentile-point gain, regardless of the socioeconomic status of the state's students.

The choices your school makes to meet the demands of the public through funding affect you and your students. Be proactive. Learn the facts so that you can be a part of the solution for your school and for your students. Keeping up with legislation and solutions is not just for administration and government anymore; we owe it to ourselves and our students to know what our choices are. Go to your government or state education Website to begin to learn about how your state is using resources. Join the professional organizations that provide journals and news briefs to you about the trends and politics of education.

SCHOOL CHOICE

Under the No Child Left Behind Act (2001), parents can make choices about their children's schools if the schools are not performing adequately. What does that mean? It means that when a school cannot show through standardized tests and other means that all students in that school are making yearly progress identified as adequate, the parents can move their children to a school that is making greater gains in achievement. The local district must provide more than one choice for the parents and must provide transportation to the selected school.

Cicchinelli et al. (2003) say that although moving children to another school may be a quick fix, it may not be a good solution over time. They provide these reasons:

- Removing students from low-performing schools does not address the underlying problem of the school.
- Moving students to high-performing schools can overcrowd those schools and thus erode much of the good that is being done there.
- The students who need to move (low-performing, low economic status, or at-risk students) may not be the ones who take advantage of the opportunity since their parents are often not as informed about school choice.

QUALITY TEACHERS AND QUALITY TEACHING

Under the current federal law, by the end of the 2005–2006 school year all public school teachers who teach core academic subjects must be "highly qualified." What does that mean? According to the No Child Left Behind Act (2001), *highly qualified* means:

- Teachers are state certified.
- Teachers have passed the state teacher licensing examination.
- Teachers hold a license to teach in the state.
- Teachers must demonstrate subject-matter competence by passing a state test or having a master's in each of the subjects that they teach.

This is a very controversial part of the act because many argue that just knowing the teaching subject does not guarantee that a teacher can be successful in teaching students. Indeed, one need only examine the reasons why teachers leave the field to discover that knowing the subject is far from being enough. In the future, look for test makers and governments to seek ways to identify good teachers through other means, especially through demonstrated ability rather than paper-and-pencil tests. Remember that pencil-and-paper tests most often test declarative information like facts, dates, times, and vocabulary, while authentic assessment more often tests procedural knowledge such as what we can do with the declarative information through processes (such as teaching).

An important part of the politics of teaching is that teachers are aware of the following:

- They are aware of their role as it applies to the classroom, to the school, and to the community.
- They are part of a learning community.
- They know how to relate to students, colleagues, parents, and the community.

- They know themselves in regard to attitudes, self-concept, sense of mission, and purpose.
- They are self-reflective.
- They are able to work with others toward school improvement.
- They are willing to pitch in and work toward the betterment of the organization.
- They stay informed and actively seek ways to grow in the profession.
- They understand that being a professional means working not only with parents and students, but with the entire community.

2

Being Part of a Learning Community

I n their book *Educators as Learners,* Penelope Wald and Michael Castleberry (2000) talk about the enormous pressure on educators today:

> In the quest for school improvement, change initiatives have overwhelmed the system. Several decades ago, schools might have had one initiative every year or two—mostly in the form of textbook adoptions. Now schools are struggling to coordinate multiple initiatives that are simultaneously stacked one onto another.

Being an educator today is a challenge that is almost impossible to meet without support. As teachers we are all a part of a learning community that includes our colleagues, parents, students, and the community at large. Some of those communities function better than others; the good ones function more like those that Mary Driscoll (1988) defines as places where:

- A system of values is shared and commonly understood among the members of the organization.
- A common agenda of activities marks membership in the organization.
- Teachers engage in collegial practices and perceive other teachers as sources of help and support when faced with academic programs.
- This same type of connection manifests itself in relationships with students.

As our public schools become more and more a place for students from the inner cities and from poverty, Karen Seashore Louis and BetsAnn Smith (1996) add that schools that are successful in these conditions pay attention to school culture, organization and leadership. By school culture, Louis and Smith include the following:

- A sense of mission. Schools that have been successful in teaching to all students have a mission statement that has meaning. Everything that is done in the school reflects that mission. This means that everyone in the school shares the belief that all kids can learn and that they will do all that is possible to see that do. What this means for kids is that if they are expected to do quality work in math, they cannot go down the hall to English and do shoddy work. The mission is that all kids can learn, and that they can learn at a quality level.

- Collegiality among all of the staff. In this type of atmosphere teachers help one another, and they share ideas and materials. There is a sense that "we are all in this together."

- Emphasis on respect for everyone including students. As Louis and Smith (1996) put it, "Caring is good for students but it is also good for teachers. Caring makes schools into ethical and moral environments, not just arenas for 'getting the job done.'"

- Teachers are problem solvers. Teachers are empowered in such a school and are encouraged to find root causes of problems and to a part of the solution. Teachers act when they see a problem rather than waiting for someone else to fix it. In turn, teachers are given a wide latitude in making decisions.
- Peer pressure to do well is a fact of life. In successful schools, everyone is expected to do their best work and to do what is best for kids. Colleagues encourage and demand excellence from their coworkers.

If you have been blessed to work in such a place, you know the extraordinary value of doing so. If you work in a place that is not quite there yet, this chapter will offer some guidelines and lifelines for you. Let's look at some of the issues that separate professionals and keep us from working as a team.

THE BIG MACHINE APPROACH

Wald and Castleberry (2000) explain that by adding more and more initiatives each year, we have created an "overwhelmed and overworked staff and a potentially fragmented education for our students." They go on to ask the question that many of us have asked: "How did education decide on this additive, piecemeal approach to school improvement?" The answer is that education was founded on some of the same principles as business and industry. Caine and Caine (1997) explain the system of education in terms of the flow of information. A simple analysis of their research goes something like this:

1. The policies on curriculum are made at the state and district levels. Standards and benchmarks are set, and tests are administered at given grade levels to determine proficiency. In some cases, students may not move to the next grade level or graduate without showing proficiency on the given assessment.

2. Administration is responsible for distributing information to be taught and assessing both the delivery of the curriculum in the classrooms and the teachers themselves.

3. The teacher is told "what" to teach but is given a great deal of freedom to decide "how" to teach.

4. Teachers assess student work and provide that information to parents and to the principal through report cards, paperwork, or other means determined by the school.

This is very much a system with subsystems within it. In industry, if there is a breakdown in the system, analysis of the system reveals where the problem is, the problem is corrected, and the system moves on. In education we deal with flesh and blood, not with things that are all alike. Thinking that all students will come down the conveyer belt at the same rate with the same wrappings is ludicrous—we in education know better. Yet in an effort to answer to the demands for accountability, we often feel we are being pushed into that model. Isolate the problem and fix it fast, usually by adding something on such as more curriculum or more staff. The initiatives under current federal law (specifically, the No Child Left Behind Act) call for educators to begin to make choices about where funds will be spent. In other words, fund what works and begin to trim off what does not. To do that we must work together as a team to make choices based on fact and on what is best for kids. As a matter of fact, in any decision we make in regard to education, the first question we should always ask is, "Is it better for kids?" If the answer is "no," we need to rethink our priorities.

What do you know about the data available in your school for making good decisions? Here are some things to ask for:

- A copy of the latest test data, including state and national test data. The data should be broken down by ethnicity, by grade level, by gender, and by special programs.

- A copy of the objectives for your state test.
- A copy of the standards for your grade level or subject matter. Most states also include benchmarks.
- A breakdown of the student population by ethnicity and by socioeconomic status.
- A list of the programs offered in your school that go beyond the regular curriculum. For example, Title I programs, Special Education programs, gifted programs, and programs for at-risk students.
- What is the policy for students who are absent too often?
- What is done for students who do not qualify for special education services, yet are not growing academically?
- What are the alternative programs for students with learning problems, severe discipline problems, or problems with drugs and alcohol?
- What kind of counseling service is available for students (and teachers)?

If this information is not available to you for all students, at least have it on hand for the students you teach.

ACCOUNTABILITY TO THE LARGER SYSTEM

As I said earlier, a school is a part of a large system and of many subsystems. It is important for all members of the larger system to work together and to comply with rules, laws, and changes in the whole system. Often teachers are given requests (or demands) for higher test scores, better use of resources, more parent contact, and the like, from sources within the larger system—sometimes from people unknown to the teacher. As teachers, we are part of the whole system, and the expectation is that we will meet the demands of the community and of the school system itself. This often leads to a sense of helplessness, discouragement, or worse, when we do not understand the demands on our time and on the time allocated to our students. Those demands often come from people outside the system, such as federal or state governments, and are important to the resources for the whole system. The key is to ask "why" rather than complaining and stewing about "another request." Information is power; don't be afraid to ask for the "big picture." As members of the learning community, we know that the system of which we are a part is much broader than the focus of one classroom or even of one person. Put simply, being a team player means that I listen to what others are asking me to do, and I comply to the best of my ability unless what I am being asked is morally and/or ethically incorrect. I have been both classroom teacher and administrator over my career. When I became an administrator I realized that many of the frustrations that I felt as a teacher could have been alleviated if someone had just filled me in on the importance of what was being done. We all need to be empowered.

To help you as you become acquainted with the big picture, here are some things that you need to know:

- The policies and procedures not only of your school but also of the district or system itself.
- How to find the state codes under which your school operates. These are usually under your state education Website, but I have found that is not true for every state. Ask for the Website address so that you can stay current. Remember that when your state legislature meets, changes usually follow. A comprehensive guide to changes is usually available from the state administrators' organizations and state school board organizations. Here is a guide to finding their Websites. The National School Boards Association is www.nsba.org. You can usually find your state division of that organization by going to the national Website. The National Association of School Administrators is found at www.nasa. Other organizations, such as the National Middle School Association (www.nmsa.org),

the National Association of Secondary School Principals (www.nassp.org), and the National Association of Elementary School Principals (www.naesp.org), are all great sources to keep you informed.

FINDING RESOURCES

There was a time when I would have written this book without much discussion on the community. We have come to realize that the community is a vital resource for schools, and it is one of the major stakeholders in your school. I live in Texas, a state with many small school districts. From time to time our legislature has talked about combining some of those small schools into larger districts. Every time that issue comes up, people in small communities become excited because if a school is moved out of a community, the community usually does not survive. By the same token, if a school does not include the community, the school has difficulty surviving. Because so many parents today work long hours and may even have more than one job, the need for community involvement has become very important.

Every community has its "movers and shakers," the people who know what is going on, the people who can lead you to resources, the people who can help you fulfill your dreams for your students. When my school made major changes in the way we teach and assess students, we involved our community in every step. We called in a group of influential people in the community: bankers and factory owners, ministers and the working people. No group was left out. We asked them, "If we could give you a better product, would you pay for it?" The answer was a resounding, "Yes." As a matter of fact, the president of a major company in our community said, "Not only will I be willing to pay for it, I will allow my workers to serve on committees during working hours to make it happen." He kept his promise, and we turned the school around to be one of the most successful in the state. We involved the community in every inservice training that we conducted, we involved them on committees, and we formed an organization called V.I.P. for Very Important Parents. If I were organizing the group today, I would change that to Very Important People because I would also want to involve senior citizens, young couples who do not have children yet, and the students (we did have separate student committees).

It was amazing how much this group took off of us in terms of workload. The V.I.P. committee took over Open House Week, and we had more people than ever before come through the schools. The V.I.P. committee took over the school prom and other outside events for which faculty had always been responsible. In turn, we opened our doors to our parents. Any parent or community member was invited to come to school and to sit in on classes anytime they wished. They had to go through the V.I.P. committee first and let us know they were coming (for safety reasons), but they were welcome. Opening the door did several significant things for us: (1) Student behavior was better when parents were around; (2) people complained less about the school—after all, we are afraid of the things we cannot see or do not know about (when we opened up the school, we took away the fear); and (3) we got tremendous parent support for what we were doing.

We also sent the standards and objectives for our grade levels or courses home to parents. As one high school student put it when she thanked me for sending home the pages of objectives for the course, "Now my parents can't say I don't do anything all day—as a matter of fact, they feel sorry for me now."

For so many years, when parents complained about school, we would dig in, tighten our hold on secrecy, and fight back. That didn't work very well; it is time to open the doors and windows and to let parents know what we are doing and why.

What do you know about the community in which you work? Do you know the following?

- Demographic information

- The map of the area that includes the school's boundaries

- Information about churches and schools (What are the feeder schools?)

- What is the average income level?

- What are resources within the community?

- What are resources within a 20-mile radius of the school (for field trips)?

- What organizations serve the community?

- What is the unemployment rate?

- Who are the movers and shakers in the community?

- What is the expectation of the community in regard to the schools?

- Who can provide services to students who need health care, dental care, food, medicine, time, or just a good role model?

WORKING WITH COLLEAGUES

Just as the climate within a classroom is important in terms of social and emotional development, so the climate of the school is important to those who work there. This includes the principal, the secretary, the janitor, the kitchen workers, the counselor, the special programs people, the aides, the teachers, and the students. No one wants to get up in the morning and face a school where people do not work together and may even work against one another. While you or I alone cannot fix a school that is negative, we can refuse to contribute to the negativity.

As a teacher, I realize that I am a part of a working community that involves many people at various levels and that all of us are important to the whole. Teachers are expected to serve on committees, to observe their colleagues, to be observed, and to work together on projects. If I think the janitor is not important enough to speak to, I may change my mind the day one of my students gets sick in my room. If

I think that my principal is just there as a figurehead, I may change my mind when one of my students becomes belliger- ent in the classroom and I need help.

Working with others means that I must first identify within myself my beliefs, biases, and expectations in regard to my job. I may be tired and not really want to attend a special education placement meeting after work, but I will be glad I did when I have an experience I do not know how to handle with a special education student.

Many graduates enter the teaching field believing that they will go home early and have holidays off. Their first dis- illusionment with the job comes about the second week of school when they are exhausted from meetings and the workload. Teaching is hard work and, because we work with people, not things, the days are not predictable, people are not always nice, and there are many demands on our time. You will be expected to work within the framework of your campus, and you will have after-school meetings and some night and weekend meetings as well.

Another disillusionment that I sometimes hear from my college students who are working in schools is that teachers do not all agree on what is best for kids. Each of us comes to the workplace with a set of ideas based on our past learning and experiences. Noted author and futurist Joel Barker (1992) said in *Future Edge,* "We will never change people until we change what they know." That is absolutely true. So, if you want to change your colleagues or sell them on a program, get facts, research data, and present your case: Change what they know.

In every school in which I have worked from the time I graduated from college until the present, I have always volunteered to do whatever needed to be done. It has paid off tremendously because I have had experience far beyond that of most of my colleagues. I have worked with students on drugs, I have attended community meetings for troubled youth, I have worked with technology from the time it was first introduced in schools, and I have supervised literally everyone in the school district with the exception of the superintendent. At some time in my tenure, I have been book custodian, public relations manager, run payroll, known which product would take scuff marks off of the hall floor, designed buildings, designed technology applications, chosen software, run the library, conducted training, taught at all grade levels, and worked with all kinds of students. As teachers we can choose to clock in and out each day, do the minimum to get by, and learn our students' names by Christmas or we can choose to be a part of the entire system and to learn every day, just as our students learn. The choice will make a huge difference in what we become.

Here are some things you will need to know:

- When faculty meetings are held
- The school calendar for students and for students. I say this because there may be dates when the students do not come to school but the faculty is expected to be at work.
- The kinds of committees your school has and what they do
- When scheduled parent meetings are held—for example, Open House, Public School Week, Meet the Parents Night
- How to reach your colleagues after hours if needed
- How you can be reached if school is cancelled. (In Texas, we really cannot drive in snow and ice. I realize in other parts of the country this is not an issue.)
- Who you should call when you will not be able to come to school due to illness or other causes
- Who the key people are to contact if you have a problem with a student, the room temperature, books, or if you want to schedule the use of other facilities within your school
- Whether there is a buddy system for emergencies, such as if a student becomes belligerent and you cannot leave the room
- How other emergencies and emergency drills are handled

The teacher is able to establish a relationship of trust with parents or guardians from diverse backgrounds and to develop effective parent-teacher partnerships that foster all students' learning and well-being. The teacher recognizes the importance of maintaining ongoing parent-teacher communication, is aware of factors that may facilitate or impede communication with students' families, understands basic principles of conducting parent-teacher conferences (e.g., beginning and ending on a positive note, avoiding technical jargon), and knows how to work cooperatively with parents to devise strategies for use at home and in the classroom.

BEING SUPERVISED

We are all evaluated on our work, whether we are the boss or one of the workers. Today, everyone is accountable. I have been evaluated so many times in my teaching career and have been an evaluator, yet I am still nervous every time. We all want to do well, to succeed. Every teacher experiences that year or that class that comes out of nowhere and it seems nothing we do works. We have all been there, and there is comfort in that fact. Talk to the people who will evaluate you so that there are no surprises. I have been in hundreds of classrooms as an evaluator and I can tell you that trying to hide a situation that is not working usually ends in disaster. I would much rather that a teacher tell me that the class at 1 p.m. is a work in progress, than have me walk into the situation unknowing. Teachers have often said they do not want to tell me their problems because I am the one who will do their evaluation.

Everyone has problems from time to time—I have had problem students, as well. If I know the problem, I might be able to help. Most supervisors feel the same way. Most of us go into a classroom looking for good things, not the opposite. I was in an elementary classroom with a young teacher who had not been teaching very many years. She was using a direct-teach method to introduce a new concept to her students. It was not going well. When she tried to start a discussion or ask questions, it was clear that the students did not understand the material. Finally, she stopped and said to the children, "I can tell by your answers and the look on your faces that you do not understand, so we are going to start over and I am going to try to explain this to you in another way." She did exactly what she should have done. The important thing going on in that classroom was not my evaluating her; the important thing was the learning. At the beginning of this chapter, I said always ask, "What is best for the kids?" If you follow that rule, your actions will almost always be correct.

These are some things that you need to know about being supervised:

- What are the criteria on which I will be judged?
- How often will I be observed and will I know beforehand?
- Will I have a conference before and after my observation?
- If I do not agree with my evaluation, what is my recourse?
- Where are the rules found that pertain to teachers and contracts in my state?
- What are the things for which a teacher may be non-renewed in my state?
- What kind of contract do I have, how long is my contract, and how am I paid?
- How does due process work in my state (for teachers and for students)?
- What kinds of information can I share on my students?
- What kinds of information can be shared with me?
- Where can I find the standards of the teaching profession for my state?

QUALITY PROFESSIONAL DEVELOPMENT

The important word here is *quality*. Professional development has gotten a bad reputation because for many years it was either just for entertainment or else was often hit or miss. I jokingly call it the "Spray and Pray Philosophy of Training." Professional development is sprayed among teachers and staff and someone prays that it sticks. Of course a one-day training on a new concept is not adequate training, just as introducing a new concept to students one day and never mentioning it again is neither good nor adequate for understanding and recall. Immersion is a good thing but it needs to be reinforced, and participants need adequate time to make meaning of the information, make it into a personal model, and store it so that it can be retrieved easily—just like the information that we give to our students in the classroom.

A teacher who is a professional keeps up with the information within his or her subject and with principles of teaching and learning in general. Teachers who do not pay attention to the new ideas on how the brain learns, for example, are setting themselves up for mistakes that could be avoided. Not to keep up is a form of malpractice. Chapter 4 of this book will offer some Websites to help you as you gain new insights. Not all information in education is reputable; know the authors and their reputations. The Websites that I provide are organizations with boards and with constituents who hold board members' feet to the fire on what is good research and what is not.

Join the professional organizations available in your subject area or grade level. They make up a great network of professionals who can offer you advice and information to keep you up to date. They also offer meetings and conferences where you can meet others who teach in your area. The networking will be invaluable to you as you work in this wonderful field of education.

In the next chapter, we will examine one of the most important stakeholders: the parent or legal guardian.

3

Working With Parents

P arents are among the most important stakeholders in the teaching and learning process. While administration and the school itself have an influence on the parents' opinion of the school, the person who makes the most difference in forming the relationship with the school is the teacher. Communication is vital if the relationship is to be a powerful bridge between home and school. Let's look at some ways that the classroom teacher can communicate effectively with parents.

BEGIN AT THE BEGINNING

Connections to parents should begin before students start school in kindergarten or first grade. Once you have your student list, begin to make contact and invite parents and students to come to school to visit.

If you are teaching a grade or subject above kindergarten or first grade, send a letter to parents to inform them of what you will be doing in their child's classroom and some of the things you will be studying. For secondary students, send home the standards or objectives for the course and some information about what students will learn and be doing in the course. Invite parents to visit and to participate. If your school has a meet-the-parents night or open house at the beginning of the school year, plan carefully and thoughtfully for that night. Be sure you have samples of student work and that you know the names of all of your students.

Make an effort to speak to every parent. Parents often corner a teacher at these events and monopolize the teacher's time. If the parents need a long conversation, politely suggest that you meet in a parent-teacher conference and set a date. Parents who come to these events expect to meet the teacher. Unless there is a major emergency, be sure to show up for these events and to be a willing participant. I bring this up because even in the best of circumstances it is not wise for parents to come to an empty room. The message is that this night is not important to the teacher. Invite parents to special events at the school such as sports events, musicals, plays, and the like. Let parents know when you will be doing special projects and invite them to participate, to help, and to judge these events.

Ways to Communicate

In this information age, there is no excuse not to communicate with parents and other community members. Set up your own class Website for those with Internet access, or e-mail them about what is going on in class. I know that we work with many students from poverty who do not have home computers. For those families, use other means of communication such as letters, notes, brochures (about your class and done by your class), phone calls, and invitations to the school. Even if the parents are unable to communicate back or to come to the classroom, they will remember that you made the contact. This will be very important when and if you set up a parent-teacher conference to discuss problems.

THE PARENT-TEACHER CONFERENCE

Parent meetings are extremely important, not just from the standpoint of problem solving but because what happens in those meetings may have long-term effects on the student, the parents, on you, and possibly on the school itself. A good parent-teacher conference takes time to prepare for and to conduct effectively. The following guidelines are offered to help you as you prepare and conduct a parent-teacher conference.

Preparing for a Meeting With Parents

- Work with the parents to schedule the conference at a time that is convenient for them. Remember that most of our parents receive hourly wages and they are not paid if they are not working. The last thing you want to do is set up an adversarial position by setting a rigid timeframe around your schedule.
- If you communicate with the parents by e-mail or by letter, give them plenty of time to set an alternate time if needed. If the parents do not speak English, and you do not speak their language, ask the school for help. It is important that the communication before and during the meeting is in a language that all of you understand.
- Remember that some of our parents and students have come to us from countries where there was reason to fear authority; try to put the parents at ease about the meeting and your role.
- Tell your principal or supervisor about the meeting.
- Let the parents know up-front the topics for the conference. No one likes to be surprised at these conferences.
- Make notes for the meeting and be sure that all statements that you make can be verified. "I think" and "I feel" do not work well in parent conferences and may be judged by the parents and student as bias.

- Think about what questions the parents might ask you so that you are not surprised as well.
- Gather data, records, notes, grades, test results, and any other information that applies to the conference.
- If you plan to make recommendations for special services for the child, be sure you have the appropriate papers, guidelines, and more, at the meeting. You might also want to invite the person in charge of the special service, if you will not be in charge.
- Tell the student that you are going to have a conference with the parents and why. (Be brief and tactful—keep in mind the student's age.)
- Ask the principal or a colleague to sit in if you fear the conference may be difficult. You might want to record the meeting; if so, you will want to tell the parents that you will be recording.
- Prepare the room for the conference so that the members of the conference can see one another and converse freely.
- If appropriate, you may want to have some sort of refreshment such as cold drinks or water for the conference. You may also want to have paper and pencil for the parents in case they want to take notes.
- According to McCune, Stephens, and Lowe (1999), parenting types tend to fall into one or more of the following four categories. Think about how you might work with each type: (1) Authoritarian: Parents are restrictive, place limits and controls on the child, and offer very little give-and-take; (2) Authoritative: Parents are warm and nurturing and encourage the child to be independent, but still place limits, demands, and controls on the child's actions; (3) Permissive-indulgent: Parents allow great freedom to the child and are undemanding, but are responsive and involved in the child's life; and (4) Permissive-indifferent: Parents are neglectful, unresponsive, and highly uninvolved in the child's life.

The Conference

- You have done your homework; you are prepared for the conference. Now, relax. You are at the conference to find solutions, find what is best for the child. What you and the parents decide may not be what they want or totally what you want, but if it is best for the child, it is the best solution. Remember that the parents are not there to make your life easier; they are there on behalf of their child and to do what is best for him or her. If you can convey to parents from the very beginning that the most important thing to you at this moment is their child, you will have accomplished a great deal. Where many parent-teacher conferences go wrong is when teachers leave parents with the impression that the child is a burden, nuisance, or threat to them personally.
- Smile and greet the parents warmly. Thank them for coming to meet with you. You may want to offer them water or an other appropriate beverage, if available.
- Begin the conference on a positive note. Talk about what is going well first.
- Do not use education jargon or make derogatory comments.
- Give your concerns in a positive and direct manner without embellishments.
- Make eye contact with the parents and call them by name.
- Provide documentation of your concerns. Facts are much more important to parents than "I think" and "I feel."
- Do not diagnose the child (you are not a medical doctor, and though you may think the child is hyperactive, you are not in a position to make a diagnosis).
- Do not compare their child to other children or siblings.
- Do not become defensive; this meeting is not about you personally, it is about the child. Parents have the right to ask, "How do you know?"

- Develop a plan with the parents. You will want to put that plan in writing and share it with the parents. You may want to sign the plan and ask the parents to sign it as well. Depending on the age of the child, you may want the child to sign also. Provide a timetable for implementation and tell parents that you will keep them informed about progress on meeting that timetable.
- If you are going to record the meeting or you have someone sitting in, make the parents aware of this from the beginning.
- End the meeting on a positive note.
- Thank the parents for being there and reiterate to them that your first concern is for their child. If you need a follow-up visit, schedule it now.

After the Conference

- Do a self-evaluation. How did the conference go? Did you accomplish the goal? What will you do differently next time?
- Review your notes and file them. It is very important to document everything. Even the simplest of conversations can wind up in court in our suit-crazy society.
- Update the principal immediately on the results of the conference.
- Write a note to the parents to thank them and to provide copies of plans that have been made.
- Make contact with the student as soon as possible after the conference so that the student is reassured that you are working for what is best for him or her.

WHAT IF?

Sometimes things do not go well in a conference. We all have had experiences when the best of intentions are not enough. Over the course of my career I have dealt with threats on my life, drunken parents, abusive parents, and worse. No one expects a teacher to continue a conference in which the teacher is being threatened or verbally abused. You have the right to call the principal, the police, or simply to walk out. The important thing is to remain calm no matter what. If a parent is screaming at you, screaming back will only elevate the problem. Take a few deep breaths, and speak quietly but firmly. At this point you want to calm the situation until you can get help or can delay or postpone the meeting. When you set up the room for the conference, it is a good idea to place your chair so that you can leave the room without walking by the parents—just in case you need help.

Most parent-teacher conferences end well and forge relationships with the teacher. It would be unrealistic, however, to think that they all will end in harmony. The most important piece of advice that I can give a teacher to help with parent relationships is always to remember that you are a professional who wants the very best for every student, even the ones who are struggling or who have behavior problems. What you do now in intervention may affect this student in the years to come.

4

What Does the Future Hold?

Two facts about public education in the 21st century are inescapable: The student population will become increasingly multicultural, and students will come from families of lower socioeconomic status.

—Karen Seashore Louis and BetsAnn Smith,
"Teacher Engagement and Real Reform in Urban Schools"
in Closing the Achievement Gap

Education has seen vast changes over the past century because students have changed greatly over the past century. Our culture has gone from a society based on agriculture and the farm family to a mix of many cultures that live primarily in the cities and suburbs rather than on acres of land. The past century also brought major changes in what we know about students and the learning process. Brain research and its enormous impact on our lives is just one of the changes. Computers and cell phones have added another dimension to our communication. What are the issues that are before us that we need to begin to address now? In Chapter 1 I talked about the sweeping changes in legislative initiatives;

in this chapter I discuss some of the specific issues about which the classroom teacher needs to be aware.

THE CHANGING FACE OF EDUCATION

In the introduction, I provided a powerful and prophetic quote from Louis and Smith about the impact of multiculturalism and poverty on our schools. Many schools struggle today to meet the needs of these diverse learners. Belinda Williams (1996) says that we will not close the gap for urban and poor students until we involve the entire community. She offers five areas in which we must invest time and resources:

Providing school-linked services for the families and community

We must begin to pool resources from government and other agencies so that services are provided to students and their families under one umbrella.

Making our classrooms culturally compatible with how students learn

Patricia Greenfield, Catherine Raeff, and Blanca Quiroz (1997) put it succinctly: "Children come to school acting in accordance with the invisible cultures of their homes and communities. Conflict arises when their behavior differs from the invisible culture of the school." For example, students from the urban setting may laugh if they are disciplined. Laughter in the face of trouble shows their lack of fear and helps these students to survive. Laughter when being disciplined, however, gets students in more trouble with teachers who do not know or understand the nature of the street. Do we tell these students not to laugh when they are in difficult situations? No, to do so might cost them their lives. What we do convey to them is that there is one set of rules for the street and another for school and the workplace. The two sets of rules help them to be successful in both contexts. When we understand that each culture has its own rules to live by and that those rules may not apply in certain situations, we are more likely to be able to help urban students.

Urban students tend to have their own language—the language of the streets or of their peers. In order to help them make the transition from the language of the street to the formal English used in the English classroom, we may need to start where they are. Let them write first in the language they know and then help them to revise their writing to the formal English used in school and the workplace. These students need to know that they are accepted and that we want them to be successful in school, the workplace, and in their neighborhood.

This is as much an educational experience for the classroom teacher who did not grow up in the urban neighborhood as it is for the student who needs to know the hidden rules of the teacher's world. If you want to know more about this topic, here are some sources of information for you.

Books

Closing the Achievement Gap: A Vision for Changing Beliefs and Practices, edited by Belinda Williams and available through www.ascd.org

What Every Teacher Should Know About Diverse Learners, by Donna Walker Tileston and available through www.corwinpress.com

A Framework for Understanding Poverty, by Ruby K. Payne and available from www.ahaprocess.com

Websites

Website addresses (URLs) change frequently. If you can't find a given site, try searching for it by name or key word at a search engine like Google or Yahoo.

www.lss.org: This is the Laboratory for Student Success at Temple University. The director is Margaret Wang, who has written numerous articles on the problems encountered by urban learners.

www.lab.brown.edu: This is the Northeast and Islands Regional Educational Laboratory at Brown University where you will find Belinda Williams, who is at the forefront of research on the urban learner. There are ten Regional Educational Laboratories in the United States, and all of them are involved in research involving the urban learner. Following are the names, locations, and Websites of the other eight:

- Appalachia Educational Laboratory in Charleston, West Virginia: www.ael.org
- Mid-continent Regional Educational Laboratory, in Aurora, Colorado: www.mcrel.org
- North Central Regional Educational Laboratory, in Oak Brook, Illinois: www.ncrel.org
- Northwest Regional Educational Laboratory, in Portland Oregon: www.nwrel.org
- SouthEastern Regional Vision for Education, at the University of North Carolina at Greensboro: www.serve.org
- Southwest Educational Development Laboratory in Austin, Texas: www.sedl.org
- WestED Laboratory for Educational Research and Development, in San Francisco, California: www.wested.org
- Pacific Resources for Education and Learning in Honolulu, HI: www.prel.org

www.nea.org: This is the Website for the National Education Association

Having Teachers Who Are Warm, Culturally Sensitive, and Who Communicate High Expectations for All Students as the Norm in Every Classroom

The key here is in the expectations. We often give lip service to "Every child can learn," but many of us do not truly believe it. When we believe it, we will see it. One of the most important gifts that we can give our students is to provide opportunities for them to be successful. Self-efficacy is powerful. Self-efficacy says, "I know I can be successful because I have experienced success before." Self-efficacy is not based on feelings but on fact. Once we help build self-efficacy in our students, we will begin to see a change in their attitude toward learning and in their motivation to complete tasks with high energy. I write about how to do this in *What Every Teacher Should Know About Student Motivation* (Tileston, 2004d). Zeichner (1996) provides four elements that are important if we are to move all students to high academic standards:

1. Truly believing that all students can succeed and communicating that belief to them.

2. Acknowledging students' culture, speech, and methods of learning that they bring with them while at the same time teaching the codes and customs of the school.

3. Self-examination of our own ethnic and cultural identities and then knowledge about our students' sociocultural development. We need to help students with second language acquisition (formal English used in the classroom and at work).

4. Teachers need more training in how to guide students into meaning making and on reciprocal instructional methods.

Providing learning opportunities for urban learners

We provide opportunities for urban learners to learn on a level playing field when we eliminate stereotyping, bias in testing and information gathering, and in sending minority students to compensatory and special education programs in disproportionate numbers. We must look more carefully to be sure that any learning problems are not caused by our lack of knowledge about the culture and background of the student.

Creating resilient environments

Belinda Williams (1996) lists traits that contribute to resiliency in urban learners: social competence, problem-solving skills, autonomy, and a sense of purpose for the future. Using Dr. Williams's list, let's examine some things that we can do to implement resiliency in our students:

Social competence—Teach students the "hidden rules" that they must understand to be successful in school and in the workplace. These "hidden rules" include such things as language acquisition, dealing with middle class issues such as discipline and conflict resolution, putting information into context, and the expectations of school and the workplace.

Problem-solving skills—Directly teach students how to set goals and how to monitor those goals to make changes when needed. Demonstrate how you use positive self-talk to walk through problems and solve them. Begin by asking your students to write personal goals for the units of study in your classroom. Model this behavior by sharing with your students and their parents the declarative and procedural goals that you have for the learning. Go back often to the goals that are written and help students to self-evaluate where they are with the learning.

Autonomy—Give students choices. When we give people choices, we empower them. Along with choices, give them frequent feedback. The feedback must be specific and prescriptive. This is much more than just saying, "Good going."

A sense of purpose and future—Many students come to us from situations of failure that have been handed down for several generations. Their overriding idea may be that there is no personal locus of control, that everything is decided by fate. Help students to see that we control much of what happens to us and that we can change our lives. Give them hope.

High levels of teacher engagement—Teachers must be actively involved all the way from bringing in resources that reflect the culture of the students to providing encouragement and feedback. It takes a great deal of energy to be a teacher.

THE MOVE TO STANDARDS

With the sweeping changes enacted by bills such as No Child Left Behind, the move to standards-based teaching and learning is alive and well. What, exactly, does "standards-based teaching" mean? In a school where the teaching and learning process is directed by standards (state, national, and/or local), all teaching and assessment are aligned to given standards. Teaching to standards may vary from school to school, but these are the steps generally followed:

1. The school faculty and administration decide on and may even participate in the writing of the standards that will be used for the curriculum of that school.

2. Once the school defines standards, teachers develop instruction around the standards set for their subject area and grade level. At the elementary level, for example, one of the strands (general topics that are a part of every grade level) for mathematics may be geometry. That does not mean that the school will suddenly be teaching students to complete the kinds of geometry problems that we usually associate with geometry but that the teachers will be teaching skills that will lead students to be able to do those problems at a later age. For the first grade, the geometry standard might look something like this:
   - Geometry: Students will learn basic geometric shapes and terms

3. Next, examine the benchmarks that identify what students at your grade level will need to know about the standard and on what they will be tested. About 85% of the state tests on standards are on the vocabulary of the benchmark.

- 1.1 students will identify squares, triangles, circles, and rectangles in context

4. As the classroom teacher, I might write the following as my objectives:

  - Declarative objectives: Students will know:
    1. The terms *square, triangle, circle,* and *rectangle*

    2. Where and how these terms are used

    3. What circles, squares, triangles, and rectangles look like

  - Procedural objectives: Students will be able to:
    1. Draw a circle, square, triangle, and rectangle

    2. Identify each of the four shapes in context—that is, within the classroom

5. Students set their own objectives for the learning. What do the students want to learn about the four shapes?
  - Students are taught using the objectives as a guide.
  - Students are assessed based on the benchmarks selected from the standards.
  - Students are tested at given intervals by the state on the standards.

CHANGING IDEAS ABOUT THE TEACHING PROCESS

As brain research has become more influential in the way we teach students, the methods that we use in the teaching-learning process have come into question. We know now that how we teach affects the way the brain processes information, and the way the brain processes information affects how well our students can recall the knowledge. We also know that when we teach processes, we need to provide opportunities for practice until a process becomes internalized. We know that if the learning does not have meaning and personal context for learners, the students will have difficulty with the learning. We also know that it is important to teach to various modalities so that we reach all students, and that if we re-teach a student in the same modality, the chances are that the student will still not understand. We must teach slow learners in the modality most comfortable for them. I like the questions asked in the Infobrief article by Cicchinelli, Gaddy, Lefkowits, and Miller (2003).

Instead of first focusing on what to do in the classroom, it's most wise to focus on how to think about teaching and learning.

- Which makes better sense to you: that you do most of the work in the classroom, or that students are the primary workers and thinkers? Why?
- Does it seem more likely to you that everyone should always need the same book, math problem, or art lesson? Or are students likely to show up at different points of readiness for reading and math and drawing? Why?
- Do students all seem to learn in the same way or at the same pace? Or do some process information differently and at a different pace than others? How do you know?
- Do you learn more about students by talking *to* them or by talking *with* them? Why?
- Do students become independent learners in classrooms where they are always told what to do? Or do they become independent when teachers systematically give them more responsibility for learning and teach them how to use the independence wisely? Why?
- Do learners care if they have choices about what and how to learn? Do they care a lot or a little? Why?
- Are we most motivated to grow when we try to reach our own ceilings or when the ceilings are someone else's? Why do you say so?
- In general, are you more effective and efficient at teaching with small groups of students and individuals, or

are you more effective with the whole class? Why do you say so?

- Is learning richer and more permanent when it's rote or meaning based? How do you know?

The Teacher as a Professional: Why It Matters

Being a professional is important to you as a teacher because it ensures your success in your chosen field. You are much more likely to find satisfaction in teaching if you adhere to a code of ethics and conduct usually associated with professionalism. This code includes the following:

Professionalism matters to your students because it means that they will have the best teacher possible and thus the best opportunity to be successful. Laczko and Berliner (2003) quote some very disturbing statistics in the article they wrote for the Association for Supervision and Curriculum Development. They say that the lack of preparedness on the part of teachers in the field affects student learning by 20 percentile points each year. That means that a student who is taught by someone poorly prepared to teach will fall short of what he or she could have learned by 20 percent each year that the student has such a teacher. Lazcko and Berliner say that we should first do no harm: Put qualified and effective teachers into every classroom.

Louis and Smith (1996) refer to this as teacher engagement. They say, "Unengaged teachers have been described as bored teachers who just go through the textbook and aren't thinking, teachers nicknamed 'Mrs. Ditto, or Mr. Filmstrip,' teachers who 'taught one year, for 30 years' and teachers who barely know their student's names." They go on to say that there are four distinct types of teacher engagement:

- Engagement with the school as a social unit
- Engagement with students as unique, whole individuals rather than as empty vessels to be filled

- Engagement with academic achievement
- Engagement with a body of knowledge needed to carry out effective teaching

How Can You Keep Up?

New advances in education come out daily. How can a teacher keep up with what works for kids, and how can the teacher know what is junk and what is not?

I am going to leave you with some great Websites that are monitored by people who are ethical and are knowledgeable about what research is worthwhile and what is not. I also encourage you to join professional organizations that provide journals, briefs, and Internet information to help you keep up in your profession.

www.nassp.org: The National Association of Secondary School Principals

www.naesp.org: The National Association of Elementary School Principals

www.nascd.org: The National Association of Supervisors and Curriculum Developers

www.nsba.org: The National School Boards Association

www.naeyc.org: The National Association for the Education of Young Children

www.ira.org: The International Reading Association

www.ncte.org: The National Council of Teachers of English

www.nctm.org: The National Council of Teachers of Mathematics

www.nsta.org: The National Science Teachers Association

www.socialstudies.org: The National Council of Social Studies

www.nas.edu: The National Academy of Sciences

The profession of teaching is now and has always been a profession of which we can be proud. Over the years we have made tremendous changes in the ways that we teach children as children have changed. Teachers are in the profession because of a love for kids and a desire to do something that makes a difference on earth. Stalin is supposed to have said that he did not need to move armies or tanks into a country to take it over—he just needed one generation of its children. We have tremendous power in the shaping and climate of what this country will be in the future. No one else on earth, not even a king or a president, has the power we have in creating the future. Just think what we could do if we became a community of learners together.

Vocabulary Summary

Academic Learning Time

Academic Learning Time refers to the actual time that a student is on task and engaged in the learning within a school day.

Accountability

Holding individuals or groups responsible for the quality of instruction and the success of students is called *accountability*.

Alignment

When the written curriculum (based on standards), the taught curriculum, and the assessed curriculum can be tracked to each other, we say there is an *alignment*.

Assessment

Assessment refers to a measurement of the degree to which students have met the declarative and procedural objectives.

Burnout

Losing interest and motivation to teach is an example of academic *burnout*.

Criterion-Referenced Test

A *criterion-referenced test* is a standardized test that assesses a student's understanding of a set of standards and benchmarks. The student competes against him- or herself to demonstrate mastery rather than being compared to other students of the same age level.

Due Process

Legal safeguards that protect individual rights, including those of parents, teachers, and students, is called *due process.*

Effective School Correlates

Effective school correlates refers to the research that has identified the characteristics of effective and ineffective schools. These include (a) safe and orderly environments, (b) high expectations of success, (c) instructional leadership, (d) a clear and focused mission, (e) the belief that all kids can learn and that students need to be on task the majority of the instructional time, (f) frequent monitoring of student progress, and (g) good home/school relations.

Formative Assessment

Formative assessment is assessment that takes place before, during, and after the learning. For teachers, formative assessment includes any information gathered about their abilities throughout the teaching process.

In-service Training

In-service training is professional development that has as its goal the improvement of the teaching-learning process.

Learning Community

In a *learning community* teachers become leaders and leaders become teachers to work together to achieve the school's mission.

No Child Left Behind Act of 2001

Signed into law by President Bush, The *No Child Left Behind Act of 2001* has broad implications for students and teachers in that it calls for more testing and accountability and proof of quality teachers and quality learning.

Norm-Referenced Test

An assessment in which student scores are compared to the scores of a norm group of the same age is called *norm-referenced*. This is different from a criterion-referenced test in which students are compared to themselves in terms of mastery or non-mastery of the objectives.

Paraprofessional

Sometimes called a teacher's aide, a *paraprofessional*, is an individual who is not an accredited teacher but works under the supervision of the classroom teacher.

Parenting Styles

McCune, Stephens, and Lowe (1999) define *parenting styles* as, "The different ways parents interact with their children, including (1) authoritarian—parents are restrictive, place limits and controls on the child, and offer very little give-and-take; (2) authoritative—parents are warm and nurturing and encourage the child to be independent, but still place limits, demands, and controls on the child's actions; (3) permissive-indulgent—parents allow great freedom to the child and are undemanding, but are responsive and involved in the child's life; and

(4) permissive-indifferent—parents are neglectful, unresponsive, and highly uninvolved in the child's life."

Performance-Based Instruction

Instruction built around evaluating achievement based on a given set of standards that includes procedural knowledge rather than just declarative is called *performance-based*. Students must demonstrate understanding rather than just repeating declarative information. Performance-based instruction includes both declarative and procedural knowledge because in order to demonstrate (procedural) understanding, students must know (declarative) the information required for the demonstration.

Planning

Good *planning* is based on analysis of the task, planning for student behaviors and learning objectives, and planning for teacher behaviors and strategies for teaching.

Professional Growth

The process of improving one's professional skills and knowledge is called *professional growth*. Since the field of education is constantly changing, teachers must be life-long learners.

Reflective Practitioner

A teacher who systematically reflects on his or her performance in the classroom and development as a teacher and then uses that information for improvement is called a *reflective practitioner*.

School Culture

School culture is the learned, shared, and transmitted norms of the school. What does the school feel like, look like, sound like, etc.?

Summative Assessment

Summative assessment comes at the end of the learning and is an accumulation of all information gathered. For teachers, a summative evaluation is the final evaluation used for hiring, for special positions, and for rewards.

Teacher Empowerment

The process of giving teachers more power in the decision-making processes of the school and in the choices made by the school is called *teacher empowerment.*

Teaching Style

The way a teacher teaches is called *teaching style.* Jensen (1997) identifies teaching styles as (1) social (these teachers value classroom interactions, they stress teamwork and group work for learning); (2) independent (these teachers emphasize working alone and are likely to rely on self-programmed instruction); (3) control (these teachers rely heavily on teacher directed learning and on student learning based on lecture and class notes).

Title I

The term *Title I* stands for Title I of the Elementary and Secondary act of 1965. Over the years, this act has been called both Chapter I and Title I. Originally set up to assist children from low socio-economic backgrounds to enhance their skills in reading and mathematics, the scope has broadened as the factors that affect student progress have changed.

Title VI

Title VI of the Civil Rights Act of 1964 makes it illegal to discriminate in any program or activity that receives federal dollars. Discrimination may be on the basis of race, color, or national origin.

Title VII

Title VII of the Elementary and Secondary Act was created in 1984 to provide help for students with limited English proficiency (this is sometimes called the Bilingual Education Act).

Title IX

Title IX of the Education Amendments of 1972 makes it illegal to discriminate based on a person's gender in programs or activities that receive federal assistance.

Vocabulary
Post-Test

Instructions: Choose the best answer or answers for each of the questions.

1. Monroe School has a planning session set for Friday so that teachers and community members can examine the school's progress in terms of alignment. This means that the group will be examining . . .
    A. Assessment instruments
    B. Curriculum
    C. Legal safeguards
    D. Instructional practices

2. The work of the effective school movement still remains with us today. Which of the following is not one of the correlates?
    A. Instructional leadership
    B. Direct instruction
    C. Frequent assessment of student progress
    D. A mission statement

3. When we assess declarative objectives, we are assessing . . .
    A. Facts
    B. Processes
    C. Projects
    D. Vocabulary

4. The time that our students are on task and engaged in the learning is called . . .
   A. Allocated time
   B. School time
   C. Academic learning time
   D. Resource time

5. The reason most teachers leave the field is . . .
   A. Money
   B. Burnout
   C. Time constraints
   D. They do not know their subject matter

6. A parent who adheres to a rigid set of rules that apply in every circumstance shows which type of parenting style?
   A. Permissive-indifferent
   B. Authoritarian
   C. Permissive-indulgent
   D. Authoritative

7. A person who works under the supervision of the regular teacher but is not accredited to teach in the classroom is called a . . .
   A. Paraprofessional
   B. Parent
   C. Special programs teacher
   D. Student

8. Ms. McComas just completed a parent-teacher conference about the behavior of one of her students in class. The student is often off task or daydreaming during instruction. The parents were not concerned and informed Ms. McComas that time would take care of the problem. Which parenting style did they demonstrate?
   A. Permissive–indulgent
   B. Authoritarian
   C. Permissive–indifferent
   D. Authoritative

9. During Mr. Walker's first year of teaching, his classroom was visited several times by his principal in 15-minute "walk-throughs." In addition, Mr. Walker was required to turn in all assessment instruments that he used in his classroom along with lesson plans. Mr. Walker's principal is involved in . . .
   A. Formative assessment
   B. Teacher empowerment
   C. Reflection
   D. Summative assessment

10. Which of the following are major categories in the No Child Left Behind Act of 2001?
   A. School choice
   B. Quality teachers
   C. Assessment
   D. Greater funding

11. This act makes it illegal to discriminate in regard to race, color, or national origin in any program that receives federal funding.
   A. Title I
   B. Title VII
   C. Title IX
   D. Title VI

12. This act is sometimes called the Bilingual Act.
   A. Title I
   B. Title VII
   C. Title IX
   D. Title VI

13. This act makes it illegal to discriminate on the basis of gender.
   A. Title I
   B. Title VII
   C. Title IX
   D. Title VI

14. Polly's state test is a test over the standards passed by her state for the fourth grade. Polly's score will be based on whether or not she shows mastery of the given set of objectives. Polly's test is . . .
    A. A norm-referenced test
    B. An IQ test
    C. A criterion-referenced test
    D. An aptitude test

15. Polly's teacher develops the classroom goals around state standards. Polly's teacher has provided a list of procedural objectives. Which of the following objectives would *not* be a procedural objective?
    A. Students will know the vocabulary terms.
    B. Students will create a graphic organizer.
    C. Students will identify the main characters in the story.
    D. Students will write a second ending to the story.

16. Ms. Alvarez has her final review with her principal today to determine the status of her contract. This is called . . .
    A. A formative evaluation
    B. A summative evaluation
    C. Due process
    D. A reflective assessment

17. Mr. Denali provided his students with a list of declarative objectives for their unit on fractions. Which of the following would not be a declarative objective?
    A. Students will understand the vocabulary words identified with fractions.
    B. Students will compare and contrast fractions and decimals.
    C. Students will work problems using fractions.
    D. Students will create their own word problems using fractions.

18. Most state tests are tests of . . .
    A. Procedural objectives
    B. Declarative objectives
    C. Intelligence
    D. Standards

19. Under the No Child Left Behind Act, teachers must . . .
    A. Demonstrate that they know their subject area
    B. Be fully certified
    C. Demonstrate their teaching abilities to a mentor
    D. Serve on decision-making committees

20. Being a good planner means that the teacher plans for . . .
    A. Student behaviors
    B. Teacher behaviors
    C. Student objectives
    D. Strategies for teaching

ANSWER KEY FOR VOCABULARY POST-TEST

1. A, B, D	11. D
2. B	12. B
3. A, D	13. C
4. C	14. C
5. B	15. A, C
6. B	16. B
7. A	17. B, C, D
8. C	18. B, D
9. A	19. A, B
10. A, B, C	20. A, B, C, D

References

Bandler, R. (1988). *Learning strategies: Acquisition and conviction* (Videotape). Boulder, CO: NLP Comprehensive.

Barker, J. (1992). *Future edge*. New York: William Morrow.

Bryk, A. S., & Driscoll, M. W. (1988). *The high school as community: Contextual influences and consequences for students and teachers.* Madison, WI: National Center on Effective Secondary Schools, University of Wisconsin-Madison.

Caine, R. N., & Caine, G. (1997). *Education on the edge of possibility.* Alexandria, VA: Association for Supervision and Curriculum Development.

Cicchinelli, L., Gaddy, B., Lefkowits, L., & Miller, K. (2003). *No child left behind: Realizing the vision* (McREL Policy Brief, April 2003). Aurora, CO: Mid-continent Research for Education and Learning.

Greenfield, P. M., Raeff, C., & Quiroz, B. (1997). *Closing the achievement gap: Cultural values in learning and education.* Alexandria, VA: Association for Supervision and Curriculum Development.

Jensen, E. (1997). *Completing the puzzle: The brain-compatible approach to learning.* Del Mar, CA: The Brain Store.

Laczko, I., & Berliner, D. C. (2003). In harm's way: How undercertified teachers hurt their students. *Educational Leadership.* May, 60(8). Association for Supervision and Curriculum Development.

Louis, K. S., & Smith, B. (1996). Teacher engagement and real reform in urban schools. In B. Williams (Ed.), *Closing the achievement gap* (pp. 120-147). Alexandria VA.: Association for Supervision and Curriculum Development.

McCune, S. L., Stephens, D. E., & Lowe, M. E. (1999). *Taking the ExCET.* Hauppauge, NY: Barron's Educational Service.

The *No Child Left Behind Act of 2001; PL 107-110 (2001).*

Payne, R. K. (2001). *A framework for understanding poverty.* Highlands, TX: Aha! Process Inc.

Tileston, D. W. (2004a). *What every teacher should know about diverse learners*. Thousand Oaks, CA: Corwin Press.

Tileston, D. W. (2004b). *What every teacher should know about instructional planning*. Thousand Oaks, CA: Corwin Press.

Tileston, D. W. (2004c). *What every teacher should know about learning, memory, and the brain*. Thousand Oaks, CA: Corwin Press.

Tileston, D. W. (2004d). *What every teacher should know about student motivation*. Thousand Oaks, CA: Corwin Press.

Wald, P. J., & Castleberry, M. S. (2000). *Educators as learners: Creating a professional learning community in your school*. Alexandria, VA: Association for Supervision and Curriculum Development.

Wiggins, G., & McTighe, J. (1998). *Understanding by design*. Alexandria: VA: Association for Supervision and Curriculum Development.

Williams, B. (1996). *Closing the achievement gap: A social vision for urban education: Focused, comprehensive, and integrated change*. Alexandria, VA: Association for Supervision and Curriculum Development.

Zeichner, K. M. (1996). *Closing the achievement gap: Educating teachers to close the achievement gap: Issues of pedagogy, knowledge, and teacher preparation*. Alexandria, VA: Association for Supervision and Curriculum Development.

Index

**CORWIN
PRESS**

The Corwin Press logo—a raven striding across an open book—
represents the happy union of courage and learning. We are a
professional-level publisher of books and journals for K-12 educators,
and we are committed to creating and providing resources that
embody these qualities. Corwin's motto is "Success for All Learners."